Fifty
Shades of
Talmud

To Radell

for delight +
enlightenment

Maggie Anton
2/2016

Also by Maggie Anton

Rashi's Daughters
Book I: Joheved

Rashi's Daughters
Book II: Miriam

Rashi's Daughters
Book III: Rachel

Rashi's Daughter: Secret Scholar
(for YA readers]

Rav Hisda's Daughter
Book I: Apprentice

Enchantress
A Novel of Rav Hisda's Daughter

More Praise for *Fifty Shades of Talmud*

"Anton takes us on a tour of sexuality within the Talmud as we see that Jewish tradition is progressive in many respects and is even racier than we could have imagined."

—Amos Lassen, *The Jewish Advocate*

"This delightful little gem of a book is recommended reading for any Jewish adult who has ever had or wanted to have sex. Non-Jews, too, will be fascinated, if not a bit envious, learning about this aspect of our religion. Indeed, *Fifty Shades of Talmud* might be the perfect gift for that non-Jewish son- or daughter-in-law."

—Nancy Kalikow Maxwell, *Hadassah Magazine*

"Anton draws on her own deep knowledge of Jewish history and writing, as well as her sly sense of humor, to open our eyes to 'texts that sound more like they belong in a locker room than in a seminary.' . . . Of course, this is hardly the first time that Anton has pushed the envelope on matters of gender in Jewish tradition."

—Jonathan Kirsch, *Los Angeles Jewish Journal*

"Jewish culture . . . embraces the joys of sex as a God-given gift and even a commanded act for procreation and the mutual bonding of the couple. In this absolutely delightful collection of Rabbinic sources, together with some funny and apt comparisons to the insights of others in words and cartoons, Maggie Anton demonstrates just how sex-positive Judaism is."

—Rabbi Elliot Dorff, Rector and Distinguished Professor of Philosophy, American Jewish University, and author of *Jewish Choices, Jewish Voices: Sex and Intimacy*

Praise for the Rav Hisda's Daughter Series, a National Jewish Book Award Finalist

"A lushly detailed look into a fascinatingly unknown time and culture . . . and a most engaging heroine."

—Diana Gabaldon, author of the Outlander series

"Maggie Anton invites us to imagine the world behind the Talmud. She populates that world with engaging characters and interesting situations. Her work also introduces readers to the history and culture of Jews in Late Antiquity. Finally, Anton reminds us that women, whose voices are largely ignored in the Talmud, were part of the vibrant world that produced the greatest text of classical Judaism. . . . Anton, as a Talmud scholar, has done herself and the Talmud proud!"

—Rabbi Dvora E. Weisberg, Director, School of Rabbinic Studies, Hebrew Union College–Jewish Institute of Religion, Los Angeles, and author of *Levirate Marriage and the Family in Ancient Judaism*

"You will not be able to put this book down, and you may even find yourself rushing off to study Talmud. So curl up in your favorite chair and savor every moment."

—Rabbi Judith Hauptman, Professor of Talmud and Rabbinic Culture, Jewish Theological Seminary, and author of *Rereading the Rabbis: A Woman's Voice*

Fifty Shades of Talmud

*What the First Rabbis Had to Say
about You-Know-What*

Maggie Anton

Banot Press
Los Angeles, California

Banot Press
8726 S. Sepulveda Blvd., Ste. D-318
Los Angeles, CA 90045
www.banotpress.com

ORDERING INFORMATION

Quantity sales: Special discounts are available on quantity purchases by corporations, associations, and others. For details, please contact the "Special Sales Department" at the above address.

Orders by US trade bookstores and wholesalers. Please contact BCH: (800) 431-1579 or visit www.bookch.com for details.

Anton, Maggie, author.
    Fifty shades of Talmud : what the first rabbis had to
    say about you-know-what / Maggie Anton.
     pages cm
     LCCN 2016930454
     ISBN 978-0-9763050-6-4 (pbk)
     ISBN 978-0-9763050-7-1 (ebook)

    1. Sex in rabbinical literature. 2. Sex in
    rabbinical literature—Humor. 3. Sex—Religious aspects
    —Judaism. 4. Rabbinical literature—History and
    criticism. I. Title.

    BM496.9.S48A58 2016   296.3'66
    QBI16-600020

Cover design: Kuo Design
Interior design: Marin Bookworks
Illustrations: Richard Sheppard

Printed in the United States of America

21 20 19 18 17 16   10 9 8 7 6 5 4 3

In the spirit of
Rashi (1040-1105)

who taught that an instructor
should begin each lesson with a joke,
because students will learn
better when they are laughing

Contents

A groom comes to the rabbi with questions about his wedding. "Is it permitted to dance with my bride?"

"No" says the rabbi. "It's immodest for men and women to dance together."

"Can I dance with my wife after the ceremony?"

When the rabbi shakes his head, the groom asks, "But if I'm allowed to sleep with my wife after the ceremony, why can't I dance with her?"

"Procreation is a commandment—be fruitful and multiply," the rabbi explains. "Mixed dancing is not."

"Can we try different positions then?" asks the man. "Like doggy-style?"

"Of course, it's a commandment."

"Even turning over the table?"

"For the sake of bringing children, all positions are allowed."

"Can we do it standing up?"

"No!" declares the rabbi, "That is forbidden."

"But why?"

"It might lead to mixed dancing."

—Anonymous

Introduction

(WARNING! This section contains historical details that may cause boredom, listlessness, or lethargy.)

For those who want to know a little about the Talmud before diving into the juicy parts, here's a short intro that hopefully answers the five *W* questions: who, what, where, when, and why. Don't worry—this knowledge isn't necessary to appreciate the main text, and you can always read this section later. So if you can't wait to get to the sex, feel free to skip these four pages.

Still reading? Thanks.

We start in 66 CE, when Jewish people in Judea (a province in the south of Israel) revolted against their Roman overlords. Other countries lost to Rome with minor consequences, but the Judean War ended in an unimagined disaster for the Jewish people—the Second Temple's destruction in 70 CE. If this weren't bad enough, the remaining Jews in Judea revolted again in 132 CE, resulting in a crushing defeat in which Jerusalem was razed and much of the population, particularly the priests, were killed or taken as slaves to Rome.

Now the Jews really had a problem. Quite a number of commandments in the Torah (aka the Hebrew Bible), especially all that boring stuff in Leviticus about sacrifices, could not be done if there were no Temple and no priests. So how could Jews practice Judaism? How could Judaism compete against a new religion preaching that the covenant between God and Israel had been broken, that they were the new Israel, that their messiah's death had replaced all those sacrifices?

All was not lost. In the north of Israel a few learned men came up with a new way to do Judaism (cue triumphant fanfare): instead of focusing on the Temple cult, Jews would focus on the Torah. A Torah scroll doesn't weigh much, nor must it be read in a particular city; Jews could take it with them and study it anywhere. Following the Torah doesn't require a hereditary priesthood; any Jew (any male Jew that is) could learn its laws. But wait—these laws are scattered throughout the Torah, someone would have to memorize the entire text to know them all. So these learned men, whom we call rabbis, decided to make knowing the laws easier.

They compiled a new book that arranged the Torah's laws by category, each in its own chapter. For example, they put Sabbath laws in Tractate Shabbat, divorce laws in Tractate Gittin, tort laws in Bava Batra. You get the idea. It took less than a hundred years, and in about 200 CE, they had a single book of sixty-three chapters divided into six sections. They called it the Mishna.

No sooner was the Mishna compiled than a bunch of wise men (maybe better called wise guys) started with the questions. Of course they did, these are Jews after all. Some had legal cases they couldn't find in the Mishna; how should they handle them? Others saw contradictions between various Mishna passages; which were correct? A few complained that some parts of the Mishna had no precedent in Torah; where did those laws come from? So the next generation of wise guys set to work answering all those questions.

And do you think they answered them?

Trick question—the answer is both yes and no. Yes, they answered the questions; no, because they also came up with new questions. Now we needed another generation of wise guys to address both old and new questions. You can see where this led, as rabbis in Babylonia weighed in as well, and each generation continued to debate the previous questions and add more of their own. Finally, 350 years later, the Babylonian rabbis collected and organized all these questions, answers, debates, and stories into 517 chapters composed of over 6200 pages. They called this new text (another fanfare) the Gemara.

The Mishna and the Gemara together make up the Talmud.

Today's Talmud is even longer because later editors added commentaries, most prominently those by medieval scholar Rashi and his disciples. Jews still study Torah, of course, but for over fifteen hundred years the go-to source of Jewish Law and tradition has been the Talmud. For we are all Rabbinic Jews now—Reform, Conservative, Orthodox, secular, what-have-you. Even those Jews who don't do Judaism, it's Rabbinic Judaism they don't do.

Fifty Shades of Talmud

It may be a myth that men think about sex every seven seconds, but it is a certainty that almost no one thinks about the Talmud. Those few who do think it's full of complicated and convoluted debates about arcane subjects of Jewish law. And they're right. But surprise, surprise, sometimes those complicated and convoluted debates concern some very risqué subjects.

For according to the Torah (Hebrew Bible), a Jewish man is both obligated to have sex, under certain circumstances, and forbidden to have sex, under other circumstances. This means the Talmudic rabbis had to use their prodigious intellects to determine those precise circumstances—how, when, where, with whom? And these being rabbis, we can be confident they left no stone unturned in their deliberations, even if the result was some very X-rated material. We can also be confident that they never imagined this would ultimately be considered Jewish canon. Otherwise we would not have texts that sound more like they belong in a locker room than in a seminary.

Here are fifty of my favorites, translated into modern English, arranged more or less by subject, interspersed with appropriate (and inappropriate) pithy sayings.

*"Better stand back, Eve, I'm not sure
how big this thing gets."*

In the
Beginning
God Created
Sex

*When once the woman has tempted us, and we have tasted
the forbidden fruit, there is no such thing as checking our
appetites, whatever the consequences may be.*

—GEORGE WASHINGTON

1 Based on the verse from Genesis (the Torah's first chapter) where God blesses Adam and Eve and tells them, "Be fruitful and multiply," the Talmudic rabbis (aka the Rabbis, the Sages) concluded that procreation was the first mitzvah, the first positive commandment. Unlike today with all our varied medical interventions, procreation in Talmudic times meant having marital relations. Which means that (ta-da) a Jewish man was obligated to make love to his wife—doing what the Sages euphemistically called *the mitzvah act*. I bet Judaism would attract a lot more converts if the commandment to have sex were better publicized.

Man is not even called man until he is united with a woman.

—THE ZOHAR

Adam and Eve were apparently so eager to perform the first mitzvah that they procreated eight hours after they were created. Here is how the Rabbis envisioned the sixth day scenario: God gathered the dust that would become Adam in the first hour and formed this into a shapeless mass in the second. In the third hour Adam's limbs were fashioned, in the fourth his soul entered, and in the fifth he stood upright. Adam named the animals in the sixth hour, and Eve became his mate in the seventh. Now things get interesting. In the eighth hour, the two went up onto the bed and came down as four (Adam, Eve, and two children—Cain and his twin sister). In the ninth hour Adam was commanded not to eat from the Tree of Knowledge, in the tenth he sinned by eating it anyway, and in the eleventh he was judged guilty of sinning. As punishment, Adam and Eve were expelled from the Garden of Eden in the twelfth hour. For those not paying careful attention, note that Adam and Eve were intimate *before* they ate from the Tree of Knowledge and sinned. Also, by giving Cain and his brothers twin sisters, this scenario explains where their wives came from.

"Uh God, I hate to bother you, but we need to talk."

If you think the previous story was strange, here's one that is truly bizarre. Rabbi Elazar (aka R. Elazar) informs us that, "Adam had sex with [literally *came upon*] the animals, but he was not at ease until he came upon Eve." According to the schedule above, this would have happened during the sixth hour while he was naming them.

God was almost done creating, but still had a couple of gifts left. God told Adam and Eve that one of these was the ability to pee standing up. When Adam begged to get this one, Eve shrugged and agreed to take the other gift if that would make her mate happy. "Fine," God said. "Now what's left? Ah yes, multiple orgasms."

—Anonymous

3 The Sages took the commandment to procreate so seriously that only one of them, Ben Azzai, refused to perform it; he separated from his wife before fathering children. R. Eliezer criticized him, stating, "A man who doesn't procreate is like he sheds blood; for the Torah verse about shedding blood is immediately followed by 'Be fruitful and multiply.'" R. Jacob then added his two cents. "It is like he lessens the Divine Image; since the Torah verse describing how man is created in God's image is also followed by 'Be fruitful and multiply.'" Ben Azzai agreed and went further by replying, "It is like he sheds blood and lessens the Divine Image." When the Sages scolded Ben Azzai for not practicing what he preached, he replied, "My soul craves Torah. Let others populate the world." I suspect Ben Azzai never procreated because, though his soul craved Torah, his body craved one of his rabbinic colleagues rather than his wife—which may explain why the other rabbis criticized him so vehemently.

Celibacy is the worst form of self-abuse.

—Peter De Vries

4 What about women? you may ask. Weren't both Adam and Eve commanded to be fruitful and multiply? Apparently not, because the Rabbis ruled that while a man was obligated to procreate, a woman wasn't. You might think this is merely one more example of the Talmud's androcentric world-view, and you'd be right. But keep in mind that while procreation is pleasurable for a man, childbirth is not only painful for a woman but could be deadly, especially back then. Thankfully the Sages not only let the woman off the hook, but they also recommended ways for her to avoid pregnancy (some of which probably worked).

The most effective birth control is a toddler with croup and diaper rash.

—KATE ZANNONI

One discussion mentioned two contraceptive methods for the woman: (1) inserting a tampon-like wad smeared with a spermicidal oil, and (2) vigorously shaking her body after coitus so the semen would presumably drip out. I've heard that this latter technique is still popular today, along with the infamous, and equally ineffective, Coca Cola douche. The Rabbis evidently knew that the first method worked because they taught, "A minor, a pregnant woman, and a nursing mother should all use it. The minor because she might become pregnant and die. A pregnant woman because a new fetus might cause her current fetus to degenerate [yes, they believed a woman could conceive again while already pregnant]. A nursing mother because she might have to wean her child [prematurely] and he would die."

Why are contraceptive sponges so convenient?
After making love, you can clean the kitchen.

—Anonymous

I find it astonishing that the Talmud also describes a sterilizing potion, "a cup of roots," that permanently prevented pregnancy. It would be great if we had one of those today, but unfortunately they do not provide the recipe. I'm not sure if this next piece of advice is for those who want to procreate or those who don't, but the Sages maintained that a woman couldn't conceive if she had relations standing up (yet if somehow she did, it was divine intervention).

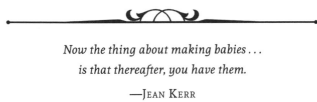

Now the thing about making babies . . .
is that thereafter, you have them.

—JEAN KERR

What's going on? you may ask. How come section number 1 has only one paragraph, number 2 has two, number 3 has one, and then number 4 has three? Congratulations, you are already thinking like a Talmudic rabbi. And you have learned something important: the Talmud is many things, but consistent is not one of them. While most of its debates reach a conclusion after merely three or four arguments, others take more, sometimes many more. Some never reach a conclusion at all.

Okay—now back to sex.

Euphemisms for Sex Organs and Practices

When God made man, He made him out of string. He had a little left, so He made a little thing. When God made woman, He made her out of lace. He didn't have enough, so He left a little place.

—<small>CLASSIC BAWDY WEDDING TOAST</small>

Every culture uses euphemisms for sexual matters, the Talmudic community included. I'll start with sexual intercourse, which the Rabbis commonly called *using the bed*, similar to our English *going to bed with*. Similarly, the Talmud's *he comes upon her* means almost exactly the same thing in English. When the Sages wanted to focus on the sanctified aspect, they referred to the *mitzvah act* or *holy deed*. A man and woman *talking/conversing* could be having sex, as could the husband who is *visiting* his wife, but if he is *lying with* her he definitely is.

Why does the Talmud call marital relations the holy deed?
Because if done well, the wife cries out,
"Oh God" many times.

—Anonymous

A man who *threshes on the inside and winnows on outside* is practicing coitus interruptus, the sin of Onan. A woman who *sets a table for him* prepares or positions herself for lovemaking. The Torah employs the verb *to know* to mean carnal knowledge so often that "to know someone biblically" has become an English euphemism. However the Talmud does not use *to know* in this way. Sadly, the Rabbis have no equivalent for our English *making love*, although I use the phrase in this book.

6 Yiddish has an extensive list of words for "penis"—*eyver, schmuck, shmekel, putz, petsl, shlong, bokher, yung, kleyner, shvants, veydl, zonef, yayzuse,* and *khalemoyed* (thank you, Michael Wex's *Born to Kvetch*). Yet despite the considerable importance in Judaism of what the King James Bible calls the "privy member," the Talmud has no specific word for penis. Yes, the Rabbis said "foreskin" and "corona" when describing circumcision, but they didn't mention the penis itself.

Men are very funny. If I had one of those dangly things stuffed down the front of my pants, I'd sit at home all day laughing at myself.

—Dawn French

Usually the Rabbis use *limb, leg,* and *foot,* just as we see when they interpret the phrase from Proverbs, "hasty with his *feet,*" to refer to improper marital relations. As you can imagine, this can lead to passages that actually denote *limbs, feet,* or *legs* sounding quite salacious. Certainly it gives new meaning to the Torah prohibition against eating "a limb torn from a living animal."

Even so, the most common Talmudic euphemism for penis is *limb*, which, unlike foot or leg, is seldom used for any other body part. For example, R. Yohanan says that "Man has a small *limb* [penis]; when he starves it, he is satisfied, and when he satiates it, he is starving." We also learn that "his limbs were shaking" means he was about to ejaculate. In one of the most egregious examples of rabbinic TMI, the Sages compare the size of various rabbis' penises. "The limb of R. Ishmael was like a wineskin of nine *kav*. R. Yohanan's limb was like a wineskin of five *kav*; others say, three *kav*. That of R. Papa was as large as a Harpanian basket."

My love comes in three sizes:
Small, medium, and fully erect.

—Jarod Kintz

A problem with euphemisms is ascertaining accurate translations. For example, one modest, yet incorrect, English translation of the previous passage about penis sizes won't even use the word "limb." It substitutes *waist* instead, which results in fat rabbis instead of well-endowed ones. Still, some euphemisms are so obvious that we do know what they really mean. For example, the Sages advise, "Do not cook in a pot in which your friend has cooked [that is, don't marry a divorced woman while her husband is alive], because not all *fingers* are the same." Is there any doubt that they're talking about the male appendages that give women pleasure, not those on their hands?

Any woman who thinks the way to a man's heart is through his stomach is aiming about ten inches too high.

—ADRIENNE GUSOFF

Interestingly, both Yiddish and the Talmud have few words for a woman's genitals; both often merely say *ha makom* (that place). Since Ha Makom is one of the many names for God, this can lend an unholy connotation to some holy texts. According to one rabbi, *kumaz* referred to female genitalia, where some women wore special jewelry (don't ask how). He said *kumaz* was an acronym for "here place of lewdness." Others said "lintel" was the vaginal entrance and "he found an open door" meant she wasn't a virgin. But she could be a woman "wounded by wood" who'd lost her virginity by some injury, not by lying with a man. We also learn that among adornments a woman made during festivals was shaving her "lower face" (pubic hair). A man, however, had a "lower beard."

Man: Want to hear a joke about my limb?
Never mind, it's too long.
Woman: Want to hear a joke about my lintel?
Never mind, you won't get it.

—Anonymous

In a debate that sounds like one-upmanship about how easily they're aroused, rather than complaints about immodest women, various rabbis defined *ervah*, which English bibles typically translate as nakedness. One fellow thought it was any amount of a woman's exposed skin that is normally hidden; others censured a female voice singing and her uncovered hair (Orthodox Jews still object to these two). R. Hisda said a woman's thigh (usually a euphemism for penis, like foot and leg) was *ervah*, but we don't know if he really meant her thighs or what lay between them. His colleague R. Sheshet was strict and said it meant even a woman's little finger. (How would he know, he was blind.) Unbelievable as it may seem today, the Sages agreed that a woman's derriere was not *ervah*, and their debate doesn't even mention breasts.

The quality of sexiness comes from within . . . it doesn't have much to do with breasts or thighs or the pout of your lips.

—Sophia Loren

9 Actually the Rabbis did talk about breasts, as we shall see, but not as *ervah*. Back in Talmudic times nobody celebrated birthdays, which presented problems for a society where different laws applied to females depending on their age or maturity. A girl (defined as younger than eleven years old) was completely under her father's authority, an adult woman (older than twelve) was not, and a maiden (between eleven and twelve) remained under her father's control until certain signs of puberty appeared to signify she had reached adulthood. In a discussion I could easily imagine happening in a locker room, the Rabbis compared the physical manifestations of puberty.

You start out happy that you have no hips or breasts. All of a sudden you get them and it feels sloppy. Then, just when you start liking them, they start drooping.

—CINDY CRAWFORD

The Sages quickly agreed that anyone, male or female, who has grown two pubic hairs is considered an adult. They next likened a female to a fig: an unripe fig while still a child, a ripening fig in her maidenhood, and a ripe fig when an adult woman. Perhaps because a fig is an obvious symbol for breast, a debate ensued with eight rabbis arguing over what kind of breast development served as additional signs of womanhood. One said the appearance of a fold across the chest, another said when the breasts began hanging down, a third said when the ring around the nipple darkened, and a fourth said when a hand pushing on the nipple caused it to sink and slowly rise again.

Men, as a group, seem to be interested in only two things, money and breasts.

—HEDY LAMARR

One can only imagine how visualizing all these budding breasts affected the Rabbis and their students. Still the text continues with four more titillating descriptions: when the breasts began to shake, when the nipple darkened, when the nipple split, and lastly, when the areola encircled the nipple. In confusion, the eight men asked Rebbi which one was the law, to which he replied, "Because we want to be strict, all of them." In other words, the appearance of any of these signs rendered a female an adult.

It is sad to grow old, but nice to ripen.

—Brigitte Bardot

10 I can't leave the topic of Talmudic euphemisms without sharing how R. Hisda, perhaps after consuming a quantity of the beer he was so famous for brewing, explained that when Isaiah warned the Israelites to "put your evil doings away . . . cease to do evil," the prophet was condemning their sexual activities. "The men of Jerusalem were lewd," Hisda began. "One would ask his neighbor, 'On what did you dine today [with whom did you lie]? On well-kneaded bread [nonvirgin] or on bread that is not well kneaded [a virgin]? On white wine or red wine [a fair or dark woman]? On a broad couch or a narrow couch [a fat or thin woman]? With a good companion or with a poor companion' [an attractive woman or not]?"

Give a man a free hand and he'll try to put it all over you.

—MAE WEST

*"God commanded us to do **WHAT?**"*

The Talmudic Sages Want Jews to Have Sex

When a man is intimate with his wife, the longing of the eternal hills wafts round them.

—Martin Buber

Honestly, how many other religions command a man to have sex? Most men would eagerly take any opportunity to get laid, and if there's no opportunity they're likely thinking about when there will be one. So how could the Rabbis possibly think men needed encouragement to perform the "holy deed"? But they must have, because the Talmud is full of inducements to do so. For example R. Akiva said that if a man wants to perform a mitzvah and profit handsomely, he should marry a woman and have children.

By all means marry. If you get a good wife, you'll become happy. If you get a bad one, you'll become a philosopher.

—Socrates

12

That sounds nice for rabbis, but these were the bad old patriarchal, misogynistic days when men wanted sons, not daughters (alas plenty of these men are still around today). The Rabbis were men, so they hoped the Talmud could help. Lo and behold, the Talmud not only explains how to have sons, it does so in several places.

If men could select the gender of their babies,
the human race would die out in fifty years.
But we'd get some incredible football.

—ANONYMOUS MALE

First the Rabbis informed us that a child's gender was determined at conception—"If the man emits seed first, the child will be a girl; if the woman emits seed first, the child will be a boy." Commentaries made it clear that *emits seed* is synonymous with orgasm for women as well as for men. How did they know this? R. Zadok explained by quoting the Torah: "These are the sons of Leah, whom she bore unto Jacob, with his daughter

Dinah." Thus boys were attributed to the mother and girls to the father. Today, of course, we know this is bogus; but if it means more orgasms for women, I'm not complaining.

13 It is also written in the Torah, "The sons of Ulam were mighty men and produced many sons and grandsons." The Talmud asked, "How is it within a man's power to increase the number of sons and grandsons?" The answer was that the men restrained themselves and delayed their climaxes so their wives would climax first. Thus their children would be males.

No woman gets an orgasm from shining the kitchen floor.

—BETTY FRIEDAN

Yes, you are reading this correctly. Over fifteen hundred years ago, Talmudic rabbis not only knew that women experienced orgasms, they knew how to make them happen. Unfortunately these texts didn't seem to be taught in rabbinic schools.

14 It's no surprise that some men couldn't restrain themselves. For them the Talmud gave another method to guarantee sons. When the Torah verse "He who is hasty with his feet is a sinner" was interpreted to refer to a man who does it twice in a row, Rava objected that this was exactly what men should do to conceive sons. The contradiction was resolved by concluding that the man should do it twice only if the woman desired it; otherwise he has sinned by annoying her.

Commentators explained that the woman would be so aroused by the first act that she would surely climax before the man the second time, and thus conceive a son. In case some rabbis missed this text, Rava repeated his advice in a later chapter. "He who wants to make all his children males should perform the mitzvah act and repeat it." Too bad for misogynistic men today; we know the Rabbis' advice doesn't work. Good news for women though; these methods may not produce sons, but they do ensure pleasure for her in bed.

A man complained to his doctor, "Help me. The man next door is older than I am, and he says that he makes love to his wife twice in a row." The doctor replied, "That's easy to fix. Say the same thing."

—ANONYMOUS

15 Women might think it's good enough that the Rabbis not only counseled a Jewish man to make his wife climax first, but also told him how to do this. Yet even better, the Talmud also taught that the man was obligated to sexually satisfy his wife. According to the Torah, a man may not diminish his wife's food, clothing, or conjugal rights. Since the Torah text doesn't explain conjugal rights, the Rabbis eagerly did so in a passage that detailed how long men with different occupations may leave their wives without marital relations.

*My psychiatrist said my wife and I should make love
every night. Now, we'll never see each other!*

—RODNEY DANGERFIELD

They taught that "conjugal rights as stated in the Torah are: for businessmen who live at home with their wives—every day; laborers—twice a week; donkey drivers—once a week; camel drivers—once in 30 days; sailors—once every six months." Interestingly, some rabbis considered Torah students to be like businessmen and others said that a scholar's conjugal obligation was once a week, on Shabbat. Of course these intervals were the minimum allowed, so ladies—if your husband neither travels nor labors at a physically demanding trade, the Talmud would have him available for your pleasure every night (and twice if you want some sons).

"I bet it's been twenty-nine days since he last visited his wife."

16

But a wife's conjugal rights weren't merely how often her husband should "visit" her. In a discussion about whether a couple should have marital relations during pregnancy, since the act was obviously no longer for procreation, the Rabbis reminded us that a man was also commanded to give his wife joy while fulfilling her conjugal rights. Rava went further and obligated the husband to give his wife the mitzvah act whenever she desired it.

Don't not have an orgasm, women. Make sure he knows that you're entitled to an orgasm.

—Amy Schumer

R. Joshua agreed, saying, "Whoever knows his wife to be a God-fearing woman and does not duly visit her is a sinner." He further stated, "It is a man's duty to visit his wife before he starts on a journey; for it is written in the Torah [that God told Eve], 'Your desire shall be for your husband.' This teaches that a woman yearns for her husband especially when he goes on a journey."

"One more thing, Moses. Taking my name in vain is swearing a false oath, not when a woman cries 'Oh God' as she's about to climax."

Jews, Both Men and Women, Should Have Good Sex

Sex is like a Chinese dinner. It ain't over until you both get your cookie.

—ALEC BALDWIN

17 The Rabbis, clearly worried that Jews weren't having enough good sex (or maybe not good-enough sex), provided another incentive: the quality of the mitzvah act determined the quality of child conceived by it. In other words, the better the sex, for both the man and the woman, the better the children. An important discussion on this topic starts with Ima Shalom, wife of R. Eliezer, explaining why her children are so beautiful. But it concludes with how bad children result from bad sex, as we see in the next section.

It is not sex that gives the pleasure, but the lover.

—MARGE PIERCY

18 The Ministering Angels stated four things: "People are born lame because their parents 'overturned the table'; mute because they kiss 'that place'; deaf because they converse during marital relations; blind because they look at 'that place.'" But the Talmud immediately negates this warning (after all, what do the asexual angels know about making whoopee?). "A man may do whatever sexual practice he pleases with his wife. Just as he may eat kosher meat salted, roasted, baked, or boiled." In other words, a married couple can do whatever they like in bed as long as what they do is kosher (this is, for procreation or to fulfill her conjugal rights).

Thus the very foreplay the angels condemned was permitted with the wife's consent: talking of intimate matters (not other subjects), looking at "that place" (her genitals) and even kissing "that place" (who knew that rabbis practiced oral sex?). Also allowed was "overturning the table," which some commentators said was coitus from behind (doggy-style) or with the woman on top, while others defined this as anal intercourse. Whatever it was, a couple might do it if they liked.

Whoever called it necking was a poor judge of anatomy.

—Groucho Marx

To clarify that they should only use the bed if the woman was willing, the Sages agreed that between a man and a woman, if she said yes she consented, and if she said no she didn't. Silence was *not* consent. Remember "hasty with his feet"? Rami bar Hama interpreted this to mean that it is forbidden to force your wife in marital relations, the result being children of bad character. On the subject of forced sex, the question came up—can a man be forced to have sex? Rava said no because an erection only occurred willingly.

A wise woman never yields by appointment. It should always be an unforeseen happiness.

—Stendhal

19 This section of Talmud concludes with ten problematic sexual circumstances that the Rabbis believed did cause bad children: (1) the woman feared the man, (2) he forced her, (3) one of them hated the other, (4) one of them thought of another partner, (5) one of them wanted a divorce, (6) they were fighting, (7) they were drunk, (8) they were promiscuous, and—my favorite—(9) one of them was asleep. (Most commentaries assume this meant the woman was asleep, but Rashi said it was the man—who would not perform well if he were too tired.)

The tenth censured situation was "with a brazen woman," but R. Samuel immediately disagreed. He insisted that "any man whose wife demands he perform his marital duty will have children greater even than the generation of Moses." The good rabbi derived this astonishing conclusion from two different Torah verses. In the first, our matriarch Leah demanded that Jacob lie with her, the result being Issachar, whose sons were "men of understanding" (along with other good qualities). Yet, in the second verse, when Moses later looked for leaders of understanding and wisdom, he found only wise men, not any with understanding. R. Samuel thus concluded that the brazen Leah's descendants were of a higher caliber than men in Moses's time.

"All right Jacob, you're coming with me tonight."

Not all the rabbis were comfortable with such audacious women, but they agreed that the woman who seduced her husband more subtly was praiseworthy. They didn't explain how she did this but like a good seductress, they left it to our imaginations. Medieval commentators suggested that the woman enticed her husband with affectionate words or adorned herself attractively to arouse his attention. One thought she should be brazen once they were in bed: "The greater a woman's desire for her husband when they are intimate, the greater their children."

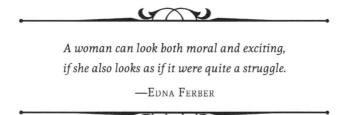

A woman can look both moral and exciting,
if she also looks as if it were quite a struggle.

—EDNA FERBER

Considering how long ago the Talmud promulgated these ideas, it is remarkable that most people today would agree that the very practices the ministering angels disparaged are in fact acceptable and agreeable, while those the Rabbis condemned are truly reprehensible.

20

In case these discussions weren't enough for a student to understand all the ins and outs of what to do, two slightly different texts inform us that Kahana, Rav's student, hid under Rav's bed, where he heard Rav chatting and laughing with his wife and then having relations with her. Kahana, unable to restrain himself, chastised his teacher for being so lustful, "It appears that Rav's mouth has never tasted this dish [in other words, Rav acts like he is starving for this]." Immediately Rav rebuked him, "Kahana, get out! This is not proper." One text ends with Kahana defending himself, saying, "This is Torah and I must learn it." The other adds that Rav behaved like this to arouse his wife. The point this story makes is that while Kahana went too far (and should have kept his mouth shut), a great rabbi's behavior, including how he performs the mitzvah act, sets an example for his students.

Laughter and orgasm are great bedfellows.

—John Callahan

And should you be in any doubt how to arouse your wife, R. Hisda advised his daughters concerning marital relations: "He [your husband] holds a pearl [breast] in one hand and a forge [womb] in the other hand. The pearl you should offer him, but do not allow him the forge until they [plural, both of them?] are suffering, and only then offer it to him." So explained Rashi. Not sure what he meant? (Don't worry, many scholars don't know either.) Here's a translation in purple prose. "He fondles the turgid tips of your heaving bosom with one hand and with his other, he caresses the intimate folds surrounding the fiery furnace between your silky thighs. He moans and presses his swollen manhood towards your overflowing volcano, until you are in such tormented desire that you surrender to your overwhelming passion and urge him to plunge in with a mighty thrust."

Some Good News and Some Bad News about Sex

I don't know the question,
but sex is definitely the answer.

—WOODY ALLEN

21 Good news—Jewish men are commanded to have sex. Bad news—the Torah forbids certain sexual relationships (adultery for example). But that leaves many details open to debate. Are certain behaviors required, permitted, discouraged, prohibited, or even ignored? Good news for Talmud students—the Rabbis must discuss all these activities and put them in their proper categories. Which means many exhaustive descriptions of sexual acts. (Hint: according to the Talmud, Bill Clinton did not have sex with "that woman.")

The way you make love is the way God will be with you.

—Rumi

2 2 The Sages taught that a man may not treat his wife like the Persians who cohabited in their clothes; in other words, a couple must make love naked. R. Huna ruled that a husband who said, "I will not use the bed unless she wears her clothes and I mine," must divorce his wife and pay her settlement. Another rabbi said marital intimacy was forbidden during the daytime; however, Rava permitted it if the house was dark and advised men to darken the room with their cloaks. These restrictions sound more like good news than bad news to me.

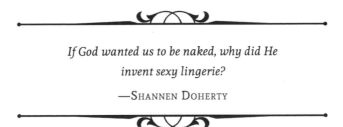

If God wanted us to be naked, why did He invent sexy lingerie?

—SHANNEN DOHERTY

23 This next restriction isn't really bad news, unless you're a rabbi who's into leather. The Sages prohibited young men from wearing tefillin in bed, even for a nap, because they might come to use the bed with their wives. (I suspect most men believed themselves young enough that this rule applied to them.) And if they made a mistake and did have marital relations with tefillin on, they had to wash their hands before removing the tefillin because "their hands have been busy." (Rashi says they have touched unclean places.)

To err is human, but it feels divine.

—MAE WEST

Here's another limitation that only affected rabbis. According to the Torah, a man who had a seminal emission must immerse in a ritual bath (aka a mikvah) at nightfall. It didn't matter if he came inside a woman or not, he was ritually unclean until he immersed. The Talmud went further and restricted the fellow from speaking words of Torah until he'd used the mikvah, which wouldn't be until sunset. This was clearly a problem for rabbis and their students, many of whom were married men who had, or wanted to have, sex fairly often. For if they made love at night, like they're supposed to, the next day they weren't allowed to discuss Torah, which was pretty much a rabbi's main occupation.

Hence a leniency was created permitting such a man to wash with water immediately. R. Akiva whispered this leniency to Ben Azzai, who then taught it in the marketplace so rabbis wouldn't neglect Torah study or procreation. Very laudable, but then why did Akiva whisper it? In order that rabbis not be on their wives constantly like roosters on hens.

Son: What is sex?
Father: When a man puts his penis in a woman's vagina.
Son: What is the Talmud?
Father: I'll tell you when you're older.

—Anonymous

24 One of the Rabbis' first tasks was to determine what constituted sexual intercourse, since this was the act with the most consequences. "Whether he only begins or whether he completes the act, whether he does one type of coitus or another . . . such is the Law for anyone who lies with someone the Torah forbids." Because prohibited cohabitation was such a serious sin that the punishment was death, the Rabbis had to establish exactly what *only begins* and *completes the act* meant. Also, since there were evidently various types of coitus, which ones did the various rules refer to?

I think it is funny that we were freer about sexuality in the 4th century. It is also a little disconcerting.

—Angelina Jolie

25 This begins a lengthy, incredibly detailed, debate that vaults from the clinical to the obscene and various points between. While most rabbis agreed that ejaculation completed the act, Rava insisted that complete copulation could not occur with a limp penis (literally a "dead member"). Though you might think every man knows what a limp penis is, the Sages still had to define it. Then they used a surprising definition—not that he was too limp to enter, but rather that he wasn't sufficiently hard that he could enter without using his hands. Thus plenty of men who thought they'd completed copulation would be surprised to learn that the Rabbis said they hadn't.

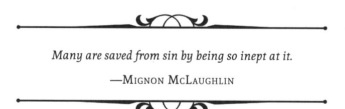

Many are saved from sin by being so inept at it.

—Mignon McLaughlin

This brings us to a disagreement over whether forbidden carnal relations while asleep is a sin. All agreed that it was a sin if the woman was asleep, but since the sleeping man had no intent to perform the act, it was not a sin if he happened to do it in his sleep (something like sleepwalking?). However, merely dozing didn't count as sleep. As for beginning coitus, some said it started with mere genital contact, others insisted that the head of the penis had to be inserted up to the corona (I warned you that things got clinical).

Last night I gave the performance of my life in bed.
Too bad my wife wasn't awake.

—Unknown

On the subject of prohibited coitus, while the Torah forbids men to lie with each other, the Talmud equivocates. For while R. Yehuda says that two unmarried men may not sleep together under one blanket, the Sages permit it, declaring, "Jewish men are not suspected of homosexual acts." Surely this cannot mean that Jewish men don't engage in such activity, since then there would be no need to forbid it. Are the Sages saying that we should not suspect Jewish men of lying with each other—the Talmudic version of "don't ask, don't tell"?

26 As for different types of copulation, the Rabbis said that the Torah verse in Leviticus that prohibits homosexual sex (you know, the one that states, "Do not lie with a man the layings of a woman"), also taught that there were two ways to lie with a woman (note the plural *layings*). These are what the Talmud calls *natural* (vaginal) and *unnatural* (anal), and the man who did either with a forbidden woman or the latter with another man, has sinned. Does anyone beside me find it interesting that the Talmud never mentions fellatio, or as George Carlin would say, the subject never comes up on the panel? Surely the Rabbis knew of it, just as they knew that generally any act not specifically prohibited is permitted.

Were kisses all the joys in bed,
one woman would another wed.

—WILLIAM SHAKESPEARE

Today's homophobes would be disappointed at how little the Talmud says about male homosexuals and that the one time it mentions lesbians their behavior is not forbidden. This is where R. Huna said, "Women who rub one another [Rashi does an impressive job of explaining lesbian practices for the naïve student] are considered like harlots and may not marry a priest." R. Eleazar disagreed, stating, "Harlotry applies only for a woman with a man; with a woman it is mere lewdness." And R. Eleazar's ruling, that lesbian sex has no legal consequences, became Jewish law. Indeed, a close reading of the Talmud shows that all nonpenetrative sex has no legal consequences.

The Bible contains six admonishments to homosexuals and 362 admonishments to heterosexuals. That doesn't mean that God doesn't love heterosexuals, just that they need more supervision.

—Lynn Lavner

27 Now we have another section of Talmud the Rabbis surely never imagined anyone would hear about (aka the long and short of it; how long does it take?) To determine how much time a potentially adulterous couple could be secluded before being suspected of cohabiting, various rabbis each related how long it took him personally to begin marital relations (that is, enter up to the corona). Their answers are enough time to walk around a palm tree, to prepare a cup of wine, to drink a cup of wine, to roast an egg, to swallow an egg, to swallow three eggs one after the other, to extend one's hand to a basket and take out a loaf of bread, for a weaver to knot a thread, and for a woman to remove a sliver from between her teeth.

This is followed by a discussion of which time is longer and which times are identical, but clearly they are all a short amount of time. If ever the reader wants to cry out TMI, this is one of those places. I must interject that people who don't read this text carefully often come to the mistaken conclusion that these times are how long it took each rabbi to complete the act, not for him to begin it. All we know from this text is that these rabbis were such a virile bunch they could be raring to go in a pretty brief time. Let's hope they wanted sons and therefore sustained sufficiently for their wives to emit seed first, however long that took.

A man had just poured himself a steaming bowl of soup when his wife came home from the mikvah. They raced to the bedroom and made passionate love.
After they'd finished, she lay in his arms and said, "Don't forget your soup." He replied, "I'll wait until it cools down; it's still too hot."

—ANONYMOUS

28 Because a wife has certain rights and obligations, and is no longer subject to her father's authority, the Rabbis had to determine when exactly a woman was considered married, not merely betrothed. Was it after the couple entered the bridal chamber or after they performed the mitzvah act? Normally these would happen in rapid succession, but not always. After a lengthy discussion, the Sages left the question unresolved, with some supporting the former and others the latter. They agreed, however, that it was disgusting for an old man to marry a young maiden or, in a surprising show of gender parity, for an old woman to marry a young man.

His friends were astonished when an elderly widower announced he was marrying an eighteen-year-old. "But my first wife was eighteen when I married her."

—Unknown comic

29 Though the Torah permits betrothal by sexual intercourse, the Rabbis disapproved so strongly that they gave lashes to men who betrothed a woman this way. Yet betrothal via coitus was legal, and since marriage was accomplished by this sex act, the Talmud needed to define it as performed for these purposes. Before going further, I want to reassure you that betrothing a woman with sex was not rape; a woman had to agree to become betrothed, no matter how the betrothal was accomplished. Imagine a love-struck couple whose fathers were taking so long to negotiate the marriage contract that the lovers impatiently took matters into their own hands. You might think that merely beginning the act was sufficient. This time, however, after yet another in-depth discussion, the Rabbis agreed that the man had to complete it. They also logically decided that a man who betrothed a woman by lying with her had simultaneously married her (that is, he needn't do it twice).

I know nothing about sex, because I was always married.

—Zsa Zsa Gabor

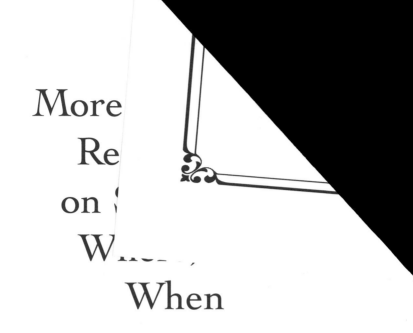

More
Re
on S
W
When

Don't knock masturbation, it's sex with someone I love.

—WOODY ALLEN

30

The Talmud takes pains to inform us of the danger of cohabiting under improper conditions. A man should not use the bed immediately after bloodletting because doing so would weaken him, nor after using the privy because the demons who lived there would still be with him. Those who did it standing up or sitting down would be seized with cramps, also if the woman were above and the man below. But if he did these things (and now that he knew about them he might want to), the cure was to chew some saffron. He was further cautioned that doing it outdoors was prohibited, even between husband and wife, unless no one could see them, and that it was rude for guests to have intimate relations in other people's homes.

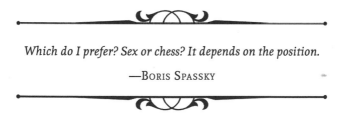

Which do I prefer? Sex or chess? It depends on the position.

—Boris Spassky

Another text warns that those copulating by lamplight would have epileptic children. Other dubious medical advice taught that the pious men of old performed the mitzvah act on Wednesdays only, so their wives would not give birth on Shabbat and cause the holy day to be desecrated. How did they know this, you ask? It was because the letters in *pregnancy* in Hebrew add up to 271, the number of days of pregnancy. When skeptical rabbis asked, "On Wednesdays only?" the text was amended to "from Wednesday onward" (that is, to the week's end).

If pregnancy were a book, they'd cut the last two chapters.

—Nora Ephron

31 Just when you might think these constraints aren't so bad, we get to Niddah, the final tractate in the Talmud, which deals with the big-time restrictions. According to the Torah, a menstruating woman, a *niddah*, is ritually unclean until she stops menstruating and immerses in a mikvah. At first the Torah's curbs on a niddah and on a man after ejaculating appear parallel—until we realize that a seminal emission is pleasurable and menstruation is definitely not.

If men menstruated, they would brag about how long and how much, boys would talk about their menstruation as the beginning of their manhood, there would be gifts, parties, and religious ceremonies, and sanitary supplies would be federally funded and free.

—GLORIA STEINEM (PARAPHRASED)

Niddah restraints are particularly onerous because the Torah forbids carnal relations with a niddah and the Rabbis extended this to seven clean days after she'd ceased bleeding. Lest you think Jewish couples only slept together half the month, consider that back then a married woman wasn't niddah all that much. Usually she was either pregnant or nursing, and babies weren't weaned for at least two years. Women who lived long enough escaped via menopause.

Judging what we've seen so far, it's not surprising that Tractate Niddah has much to say about sex, and not just concerning women who may or may not be menstruating. We do get one leniency: wives of caravan drivers, itinerant laborers, and men returning from a journey are presumed to be clean for their husbands (along with wives of any man who's been away for a while). Rabbis are men, too, and surely were well aware that niddah restrictions were the last thing horny husbands would consider when they finally got home.

32 Yet the Sages could be unbelievably obtuse, as we see in the following text. "If he was lying with a woman, and she told him she had become niddah, and he withdrew immediately, he must nevertheless bring a sin offering because his exit is just as pleasurable as his entry." Never mind how the woman ascertained this right in the middle of making love and why on earth she would inform her husband at such an inopportune moment. The important concern for the Rabbis was a man's remedy, which was that to avoid sinning, he must lie there and not withdraw until he became limp. Really? And was the woman supposed to just lie there too? Wait, the Talmud didn't say anything about her (as usual). So perhaps she could move all she liked while he lay still; eventually he'd climax and become limp, after which he could withdraw. Sounds like a better plan to me.

Over half the world menstruates at one time or another, but you'd never know it. Isn't that strange?

—Margaret Cho

33 Admittedly, this last scenario, like quite a few the Talmud deals with, was highly unlikely. Unfortunately the next problem was so common that, as an old saying goes, "Everyone either does it or lies about not doing it." Not every discussion in this tractate dealt with menstruation, or even women, for the Sages taught: "Every woman whose hand frequently examines herself is praiseworthy, but a man whose hand inspects himself, let it be cut off." In other words, the Rabbis commended the woman who often checked for blood because she would not cause her husband to sin by lying with her when she was niddah. The man was condemned because frequently handling his penis led to arousal and ultimately to (cue ominous music) "wasting seed." The Rabbis were so determined to prevent masturbation that they prohibited a man from touching his penis even to urinate, never mind any damage to his shoes.

We have reason to believe that man first walked upright to free his hands for masturbation.

—Lily Tomlin

As a further warning, R. Yohanan threatened, "Whoever wastes seed is liable to death" (at the hand of Heaven, not by a human court)—a sure sign that while the Rabbis railed against masturbation, there wasn't much they could do to prevent it. They could warn, however, against looking at things likely to cause sexual arousal. Thus we read that the Torah verse "Guard yourself from every evil thing; if anyone has become unclean by a nocturnal emission" teaches that a man should not gaze at a beautiful woman, even if she is unmarried, nor at a married woman, even if she is ugly, nor at women's undergarments. Also he shouldn't watch animals mating.

Lead me not into temptation; I can find the way myself.

—Rita Mae Brown

Tangential to the subject of niddah, we come across more disagreement about marital intimacy in the daytime. We have already seen some sages prohibit it, but here we learn that certain rabbis found it praiseworthy because a woman could easily examine herself to ensure she was not niddah, and others because the man would perform better if he weren't sleepy. I'll vote for the latter.

34 Clearly some men didn't like being told they couldn't have sex whenever they wanted (no surprise here), so the Rabbis provided two apologetics to justify why a niddah was forbidden to her husband and why a couple had to wait seven days after a son's birth to resume marital relations (as a woman, I would think this one was obvious). "Why did the Torah ordain that menstrual impurity lasts seven days? Because being in frequent contact with his wife, a husband might lose his desire for her. The Torah therefore ordained: Let her be unclean and forbidden to her husband for seven days so [when they are permitted to resume marital relations] she will be as beloved by him as in their bridal chamber."

And "why does the Torah ordain that with a male child the mother is clean after seven days and that we circumcise him on the eighth day? So that the guests shall not enjoy themselves while his father and mother are sad." In other words, if the mother were still unclean when her son was circumcised, everyone else would be partying at the banquet in his honor, yet she and her husband would be forbidden to use the bed (and thus not even allowed to touch each other).

Marriage is popular because it combines the maximum of temptation with the maximum of opportunity.

—George Bernard Shaw

After this, the Rabbis asked more questions about carnal relations. Here's my favorite: "Why does the man lie facing downward and the woman facing upward? Because he faces the place [*ha makom*] from which he was created [the earth] and she faces that from which she was created [the man]." I have no doubt that the *ha makom* pun was intentional.

35 In addition to bedding a niddah, bestiality and male homosexual copulation were also sins punishable by death. So the Talmud provides a comprehensive discussion, with way TMI, on exactly what constituted these last two acts. Just as forbidden sex with a woman occurred with the initial stage of intercourse, so it did with a man or beast. While a man could lie with an animal either of two ways, like with a woman, the Talmud assumed there was only one way for a man to lie with another man. Thus oral sex wasn't sex.

I don't even want to imagine how this next subject came up, but the Rabbis agreed that lying with a dead woman wasn't sex either. No matter how disturbing, the text implies that necrophilia might be permitted, or at least it wasn't a sin.

I regret to say that we of the FBI are powerless to act in cases of oral-genital intimacy, unless it has in some way obstructed interstate commerce.

—J. EDGAR HOOVER

Just when we think the Talmud has covered every possibility, one student asked, "What is the law if a man commits the beginning of copulation with himself." At first his teacher rejected this question as ridiculous because the act was physically impossible, but another rabbi pointed out that a well-endowed man could do it with a limp member. Again I'm amazed that while the Rabbis were perfectly willing to consider this truly far-fetched scenario, they never asked about fellatio. Meanwhile this incredible discussion eventually concluded with two opinions: (1) If a man isn't liable for engaging in prohibited sex with a limp member, then this fellow hasn't sinned. (2) But if he is liable, limp or erect, then he has committed two sins—one for performing the forbidden act and another for receiving it. Ouch, two sins for the price of one. By the way, before you dismiss this situation as a rabbinic absurdity, I have been informed by a reliable source that there are pornographic films showing this exact feat.

"The Good Inclination may be good,
but the Evil Inclination is very good."

The Evil Inclination (*Yetzer Hara*) and How to Control It

God told Adam, "I've got good news and bad news." Adam wanted the good news first, so God said, "I've given you two new organs: a brain so you can be smart and invent new things and a penis so you can have children and populate the world." Adam agreed that these were good and then asked for the bad news. God sighed. "I created you with only enough blood for one to operate at a time."

—UNKNOWN

36

The Talmudic rabbis blamed man's powerful sexual urges on something called the *Yetzer Hara*, usually translated as the "Evil Inclination." Yet they also taught: "'And God saw all that He had made, and found it very good'—*good* refers to the Good Inclination [Yetzer Hatov] and *very good* refers to the Evil Inclination [Yetzer Hara]. But how could the Evil Inclination be very good? Because were it not for the Yetzer Hara no one would build a house, take a wife, give birth, or engage in commerce."

When passion burns in you, remember you were given it for a good reason.

—Hasidic saying

This conflicted view is affirmed in a story where, after the Israelites complain that they want neither the Yetzer Hara nor the reward for conquering it, the Yetzer Hara is handed over to them. But the Yetzer Hara warns that if they kill it, the world will become desolate. They prudently imprison it for three days, during which not a single egg is laid in Israel. So instead of killing the Yetzer Hara, they blind it, with the result that a man is rarely aroused by his mother or sister. The Rabbis liked this story so much that they retold it in another chapter. That's the Yetzer Hara—can't live with it, can't live without it.

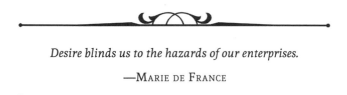

Desire blinds us to the hazards of our enterprises.

—MARIE DE FRANCE

37 Women also have a Yetzer Hara, for we learn that "while one cup of wine is becoming to a woman, two result in her disgrace, three cups cause her to solicit her husband in public, and after four she solicits even a donkey in the street and is not particular." R. Joshua agreed, declaring that women preferred poverty with sexual intimacy over riches with abstinence. But when other rabbis started to debate whether men or women have the greater Yetzer Hara, they were quickly silenced by R. Chiya, who said, "Go learn from the harlot marketplace—who hires whom?"

Desire is in men a hunger, in women only an appetite.

—MIGNON MCLAUGHLIN

"Your place or mine?"

Speaking of harlots, according to the Rabbis, the biblical harlot Rahav was so beautiful that she inspired lust merely with her name, as we learn: "Whoever says 'Rahav, Rahav' will immediately ejaculate." After R. Yohanan protested that he said this and nothing happened, R. Yitzhak explained this only applied to men who have seen her (commentators say he meant men who have bedded her).

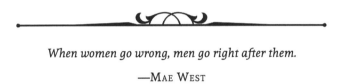

When women go wrong, men go right after them.

—Mae West

38

Conceding that a man's Yetzer Hara is stronger, the Rabbis wondered why. A rather odious comment sums up men's dilemma: "Though a woman is like a leather wineskin full of excrement and its mouth [her womb] is full of blood, even so all men chase after her." While this is a somewhat accurate physiological description of the female body, it is not how most men envision women. Thankfully a sweeter text asks: "Why do men pursue women and women do not pursue men? This is like someone who has lost something. Who goes in search of what? He who lost the thing [in this case Adam's rib from which Eve was formed] searches for what he lost."

One story details the Yetzer Hara at its strongest and most dangerous. "A man developed a passion for a certain woman, and his heart was so consumed by burning desire that his life was in danger. The doctors said, 'His only cure is to lie with her.' The Sages replied: 'Let him die rather than that she submit.' Then the doctors recommended that she stand naked before him, to which the Sages answered, 'Better let him die.' So the doctors suggested, 'Let her talk with him from behind a screen' and the Sages again objected, 'Better let him die.'" Two rabbis disputed whether she was married or unmarried. Now, it is understandable if she were married, but why such severity if she were unmarried? Let him marry her. Evidently she did not want to marry him, and the Rabbis did not countenance daughters of Israel being thus debauched.

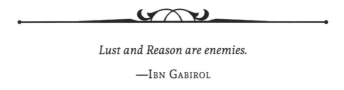

Lust and Reason are enemies.

—Ibn Gabirol

39 A wife's importance in empowering a man to control his Yetzer Hara is acknowledged in a text where we learn that when two of the greatest Talmudic sages, Rav and R. Nachman, traveled as judges to faraway towns, they married women there for as little as one night to avoid sin (of course each also had a wife back home). But some objected, saying, "A man with a wife, even if she is not with him, is like having bread in his basket; his hunger pangs are tolerable because he knows a meal awaits him at home." Still, the rabbis who compiled the Talmud thought the story of R. Nachman taking a wife for a day was worth telling again in another section.

King Solomon had a thousand wives; so the odds were good that one of them wouldn't have a headache.

—ANDY BEAL

40

Even great rabbis could be overcome by the Yetzer Hara, especially if they were overly pious. The Talmud gives us one example where the rabbi saves himself, one where Satan reluctantly saves him, and the last where the rabbi gives in but is still saved from sin.

R. Amram the Pious housed some captive women in his attic. At night one of them walked in front of a lamp, silhouetting her form. Enthralled, R. Amram set up a ladder that ten men could not lift and began ascending. Halfway up, he cried out, "A fire at Amram's!" so his colleagues would come and stop him. He accepted their reprimand, saying, "Better I be shamed in this world than in the next."

R. Akiva used to scoff at sinners, so Satan appeared to him as a beautiful woman at the crown of a tall palm tree. R. Akiva immediately began climbing up to reach her, but when he got almost to the top Satan revealed himself, leaving a mortified and chastened Akiva to get down on his own.

R. Chiya would pray, "Merciful One, save us from the Yetzer Hara." One day his wife heard him and wondered why he would pray this when he hadn't shared her bed for years. So she adorned herself and paraded in front of where he was studying. Thinking her a harlot, he propositioned her, and she asked for a pomegranate from the uppermost branch. He brought it down and had his way with her. When he got home, his wife was singing as she lit the hearth, and overcome with guilt, he sat in it. "What are you doing?" she cried out, and he told her what had happened. "But it was me." She showed him the pomegranate. "Even so," he said, "My intent was evil."

He is lost who is possessed by carnal desire.

—MAHATMA GANDHI

41 The Talmud devotes a lengthy discussion to disparaging the Yetzer Hara. R. Assi said, "First it is like a spider's web, but ultimately becomes like a carter's rope," Abaye said it incited Torah scholars above all others, Elijah the Prophet said "The greater the man, the greater his Yetzer Hara," and Rava said "At first it is called a traveler, then a guest, until at last it is master of the house." Then comes one of my favorite Talmud quotes, attributed to R. Yohanan: "Man has a small limb; when he starves it he is satisfied, and when he satiates it he is starving." I like this saying so much I had to put it in again.

The natural man has only two primal passions,
to get and beget.

—William Osler

42 Ultimately the Sages were realistic enough to understand that even a married Torah scholar might not be able to control himself. Thus they taught, "If a man sees that his Yetzer Hara is overwhelming him, he should go to a place where he is not known, dress in black, and do what his heart desires. But he should not desecrate Heaven's Name openly." In other words, if a rabbi must sin, he should do it secretly so people won't think Judaism permits this. The maxim evidently bears repeating, for we find it in two other chapters.

Women need a reason to have sex. Men just need a place.

—Billy Crystal

"No problem, they're from Judea."

Virginity, Impotence Tests, and Other Wedding Miscellany

*Marriages may be made in Heaven but
the details are worked out on earth.*

—GLORIA PITZER

43 Even so, the best protection from the Yetzer Hara was marriage, and that necessitated a big fat Jewish wedding. In Talmudic times these were lavish feasts open to the entire community, with unending barrels of wine and beer, where inebriated guests often didn't stagger home until dawn. As one can imagine, the merriment could get so vulgar that the Rabbis objected, "Everyone knows why a bride enters the bridal canopy [to consummate the marriage], but anyone who perverts his voice about this will have a good Heavenly judgment reversed." This rude behavior so upset the Sages that they reiterated their disgust in a different chapter. "All know for what purpose a bride enters the bridal chamber, but whoever disgraces his mouth with obscene words, even if years of happiness were decreed for him, they will become years of woe."

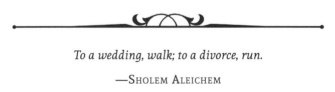

To a wedding, walk; to a divorce, run.

—SHOLEM ALEICHEM

Evidently the offended rabbis couldn't stop the popular salacious jokes and ballads, often incorporating verses from the biblical Song of Songs—all they could do was threaten divine punishment. It's too bad they didn't provide a few examples of these objectionable ditties, although I imagine that one may have been what R. Hisda said about Jerusalem's lewd men (see section 10 on page 31).

44 Most weddings were indeed worthy of celebration, but not all. In one scenario a rabbi goes into the bridal chamber to help the impotent bridegroom, his son. The text doesn't say how, and I can't imagine who would be more unwelcome in the marital bedroom than one's father. Perhaps he advised consuming some foods the Sages said cause a seminal emission, though I suspect that the Talmud was more interested in warning that these foods should be shunned to avoid wasting seed. One sage said fine flour, eggs, and white wine, another added milk and cheese, a third added fatty meat and fish, and the last garlic, cress, and purslane. The only ingredient they agreed on was eggs—which does make sense.

What's the difference between anxiety and panic?
Anxiety is when, for the first time, a man can't do it a
second time. Panic is when, for the second time,
he can't do it the first time.

—Anonymous

45 If the groom's father couldn't help, the wife was entitled to a divorce. According to Jewish Law, a man must divorce his wife and pay her a settlement if she claimed he was impotent. She used the euphemism "Heaven is between him and me" (meaning Heaven knows what really happened in their bed) to show that she was too modest to give details in court. But the Rabbis had to be explicit to judge properly, and after much discussion they ruled that a man was considered impotent unless his semen "shoots like an arrow." So no matter how hard his erection, no matter if he does ejaculate, if his wife declares that it doesn't shoot like an arrow (amazingly the Rabbis said that she, not he, ascertained this), he must divorce her. A rare small victory for women's rights.

Impotence is a man's brain saying to his body,
"No hard feelings."

—Anonymous

Impotence was such a serious charge that some rabbis preferred to test the man rather than rely on his wife's word. In a piece of Talmud so obscene I never quote it in public, Rava asked how to determine impotence and received two replies. The first was to bring hot barley bread and place it on the man's anus, which should cause him to discharge semen. Is this wild or what? Who devised such a bizarre test, and however did they know it worked? Why not hire a harlot and have her use her expertise? No wonder Abaye protested, "Is every man as holy as our patriarch Jacob, who never emitted seed until he married Leah at age eighty-four, that we go to such lengths?" Clearly not, because Abaye suggested showing him women's colored undergarments instead. Rava then objected to this second test, "Is every man then so depraved that he will ejaculate merely upon viewing women's underclothes?" Rava had a point. True that plenty of men today have gotten off perusing Victoria's Secret catalogues, but that underwear is displayed on real women's bodies. Ultimately the Rabbis decided that the hot bread procedure was the correct one, although we never hear of anyone being tested this way.

46 The Talmud spends more time discussing another wedding night problem—the bride who is not a virgin. One passage details several cases where grooms claimed their brides were not virgins (they found an *open door*), all of which were resolved against the men. One judge went so far as to lash a groom with palm switches, since only a man who frequented harlots would be such an expert on the lack of virginity.

It is one of the superstitions of the human mind to have imagined that virginity could be a virtue.

—Voltaire

"I hope we get some to drink when this is over."

Another judge employed a wine-barrel test for virginity. He brought two handmaids, one a virgin and one not, and sat them each on an open wine barrel (nobody wore underpants back then). The nonvirgin's breath became fragrant with wine, while the virgin's breath did not. Thus when the bride sat and her breath did not smell, the judge declared her a virgin. I can't help but wonder if the judge knew very well the test didn't work and arranged the outcome by secretly having the nonvirgin drink some wine first.

Here's another excuse for finding an "open door." The Rabbis acknowledged that many men were able to enter "at an angle" without breaking the hymen, and perhaps the groom had done so inadvertently. Indeed the great sage Shmuel declared himself "able to copulate many times with virgins without making them bleed." Isn't it interesting that despite the Sages' usual zeal for asking questions, nobody challenged this, chastised Shmuel for such licentiousness, or asked how he did it?

47 Not all first-time brides were virgins, particularly in Judea where grooms were welcome to stay at their fathers-in-law's homes after betrothal (but before the wedding). This practice seems to have been common enough that the Talmud mentions, without condemnation, certain rabbis' daughters who were pregnant under the bridal canopy, likely gotten that way by the groom. The Rabbis also knew that some brides broke their hymen with a finger beforehand, apparently to avoid pain and bleeding on their wedding night.

Women say they lost their virginity;
but most of them know who got it.

—Unknown

48 Losing one's virginity might be fun and games for men, but to their credit the Sages were well aware that using the bed the first time could be painful for a woman, especially if she were unwilling. Even more to the Rabbis' credit, they treated a sexual assault victim the same as anyone else injured during an attack. They did not hold her responsible for somehow encouraging the assault (for example, how she dressed or where she walked). The rapist, like other assailants, had to pay compensation for her medical expenses, time she was unable to work, any permanent impairment, her shame and embarrassment, and the pain she suffered. While deciding how much a rapist paid his victim as recompense for pain, one rabbi proposed none at all since the maiden would ultimately have suffered the same pain on her wedding night. But his idea was angrily rejected because, the Talmud declared, "There is no comparison between losing her virginity under the bridal canopy and losing it on a dung heap." (At least one would hope not.)

Bad judgment and carelessness are not punishable by rape.

—P<small>EARL</small> C<small>LEAGE</small>

Yet a virgin bride does suffer pain, and inquiring rabbinic minds wanted to know how much. This led to an astonishing passage where two rabbis asked their wives, and one asked his mother, how it felt in the bridal chamber. Talk about awkward—imagine asking your mom about her first time. Or maybe more awkward—asking your wife, previously a widow, about being deflowered by her first husband. Anyway, the three answers were "like hot water on a bald head, like the prick of the bloodletter's lancet, and like a hard crust rubbing your palate." In other words, the commentators tell us, the bride's pain is tolerable if she also has pleasure. Which is the very premise of the erotic novel my title parodies.

Speaking of bedding a virgin, the Rabbis believed that a woman couldn't conceive from her first cohabitation; maybe they assumed that women who did conceive so quickly had married men who knew how to make sons. In this final piece of TMI about virginity, the Sages ruled that a husband rendered his wife a nonvirgin with anal copulation; I suppose that means he consummated the marriage. But with other men a virgin remained a virgin after anal copulation because her hymen was still intact. That's Talmudic logic for you.

"I never imagined that Heaven would be so—well, heavenly."

At the End

That would be a good thing to cut on my tombstone:
Wherever she went, including here, it was
against her better judgment.

—DOROTHY PARKER

49 As part of a discussion of who was responsible when a man or animal died from overwork, the Rabbis ruled that a man who died from overindulgence in a brothel had no claim against the women or brothel owner. Too bad for the man's heirs that they couldn't claim damages, but at least they could hope he died happy.

An elderly man died while making love; his widow said, "He came and he went."

—Unknown

An aged R. Shimon complained, "I am old. From one who used to walk on two, I have become one who walks with three [he needs a cane], and that which used to promote peace in the home has ceased [he is now impotent]." Here's another bittersweet musing, this on the importance of love for good sex. "When our love was strong we could have lain together on the edge of a sword; now that it is weak, a bed sixty cubits wide is not enough for us."

50 There is a tradition that Torah/Talmud study should not end with an unhappy or derogatory text. In that spirit, I conclude with the possibility that there is sex after death, despite what some sages believe. For we learn that "Three things [in this world] are a semblance of the World to Come: Shabbat, sunshine, and *using the bed.*" Now, if *using the bed* is merely a semblance of Paradise, just imagine what pleasures must await us there.

I have a wife, you have a wife, we all have wives.
We've had a taste of Paradise.

—SHOLEM ALEICHEM

Biblical and Talmudic References

1. Genesis 1:28, Berachot 10a
2. Sanhedrin 38b, Yevamot 63a
3. Yevamot 63b, Genesis 9:6–7
4. Yevamot 65b, Ketubot 37a, Ketubot 39a, Shabbat 111a, Sanhedrin 37b
5. Berachot 57b, Berachot 62a, Yevamot 62b, Yevamot 53b, Yevamot 63b, Nedarim 20b
6. Eruvin 100b, Sanhedrin 107a, Niddah 13a, Pesachim 112a, Genesis 9:4
7. Shabbat 64a
8. Gittin 70a, Niddah 43a, Berachot 24a
9. Niddah 46–47
10. Shabbat 62b
11. Pesachim 112b
12. Berachot 60a, Niddah 31a, Genesis 46:15
13. I Chronicles 8:40
14. Eruvin 100b, Proverbs 19:2
15. Exodus 21:10, Ketubot 61b
16. Pesachim 72b, Yevamot 62b, Genesis 3:16
17. Nedarim 20a–b
18. Kiddushin 13a, Yevamot 53b–54a
19. Nedarim 20b
20. Berachot 62a, Hagigah 5b, Shabbat 140b
21. Yevamot 53b

22. Ketubot 48a
23. Sukkah 26b, Berachot 20b, Berachot 22a
24. Shabbat 62b
25. Yevamot 55b, Yevamot 54a, Kiddushin 82a
26. Leviticus 20:13, Yevamot 76a
27. Ketubot 56a
28. Sotah 4a
29. Deuteronomy 24:1, Kiddushin 10a
30. Gittin 70a, Sanhedrin 46a, Ketubot 65a, Pesachim 112b, Niddah 38a
31. Leviticus 15:19–24, Leviticus 18:19
32. Shevuot 17b
33. Niddah 13a, Avoda Zara 20a–b, Deuteronomy 23:10, Niddah 16b
34. Niddah 31b
35. Sanhedrin 55a, Sotah 20a
36. Genesis Rabbah 9:7, Yoma 69b, Sanhedrin 64a
37. Ketubot 65a, Joshua 2:1, Megillah 15a
38. Shabbat 152a, Niddah 31b, Sanhedrin 75a
39. Kiddushin 29b, Yoma 18b, Yevamot 37b
40. Kiddushin 81b
41. Sukkah 52a–b
42. Moed Katan 17a, Hagigah 16a, Kiddushin 40a
43. Berachot 2a, Shabbat 33a
44. Berachot 25b, Yoma 18a
45. Nedarim 91a, Yevamot 76a
46. Ketubot 10a–b, Ketubot 6b, Niddah 64a–b
47. Ketubot 12a, Yevamot 34b
48. Moed Katan 8b, Ketubot 39b, Yevamot 34a
49. Shabbat 152a, Sanhedrin 7a, Bava Metzia 97a
50. Berachot 57b

About the Author

Maggie Anton was born Margaret Antonofsky in Los Angeles, California, where she still resides. Raised in a secular household, she grew up with little knowledge of her Jewish religion. All that changed when she entered college and discovered Judaism as an adult, which began a lifetime of Jewish education, synagogue involvement, and ritual observance. This was in addition to working full-time as a clinical chemist for Kaiser Permanente for over thirty years.

In 1992 Anton joined a women's Talmud class where, to her surprise, she fell in love with Talmud, a passion that has continued unabated for over twenty years. Intrigued that the great Jewish scholar Rashi had no sons, only daughters, Anton started researching the family. Thus her award-winning trilogy, *Rashi's Daughters*, was born, to be followed by National Jewish Book Award finalist *Rav Hisda's Daughter: Apprentice* and its sequel, *Enchantress*.

Still studying women and Talmud, Anton has lectured throughout North America and Israel about the history behind her novels. You can follow her blog and contact her at her website, www.maggieanton.com.